Christmas Joy

ALSO BY MEL LAWRENZ

How to Understand the Bible (WordWay, 2014)

Life After Grief (WordWay, 2015)

Overcoming Guilt and Shame (WordWay, 2015)

Spiritual Influence: The Hidden Power Behind Leadership (Zondervan, 2012)

I Want to Believe: Finding Your Way in An Age of Many Faiths (Regal, 2007)

Whole Church: Leading from Fragmentation to Engagement (Jossey-Bass/Leadership Network, 2009)

Patterns: Ways to Develop a God-Filled Life (Zondervan, 2003)

Putting the Pieces Back Together: How Real Life and Real Faith Connect (Zondervan, 2005)

For more resources:

www.WordWay.org

and

www.TheBrookNetwork.org

Facebook: thebrooknetwork

Twitter: mellawrenz

Do you ever wish you understood the Bible better?

Almost everyone does. Mature believers and new believers. Young and old. Those who have read the Bible for years and those just starting out.

How to Understand the Bible: A Simple Guide, will help you gain an overall perspective on the flow and meaning of Scripture. It addresses questions like: What is the big picture of the Bible? What about Bible translations? How should we understand the stories of the Old Testament? How should we interpret what the prophets had to say? How should we understand the teachings of Jesus? What was Jesus teaching in the parables? How can we hear God's voice in Scripture? What are the proper ways to apply Scripture to life today? Available at Amazon.com.

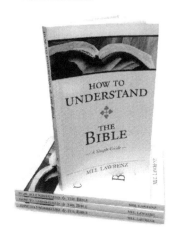

CHRISTMAS JOY

MEL LAWRENZ

WWW.WORDWAY.ORG

WordWay
Christmas Joy
Copyright © 2014 Mel Lawrenz
This title is available as a Kindle ebook.
Requests for information should be addressed to:
WordWay Resources P.O. Box 231, Waukesha, WI 53186

Published by WordWay Resources LLC
www.wordway.org

All Scripture quotations, unless otherwise indicated, are taken from The Holy Bible, New International Version. Copyright © 1973, 1978, 1984, 2011, by Biblica, Inc.

Cover and interior design: Sheila Hahn

CONTENTS

To the Reader

The days leading up to Christmas present us with an extraordinary opportunity for us to grow in our knowledge of Jesus the Christ, who called himself the way, the truth, and the life. On many occasions Jesus told his followers reasons why he came. Ordinary people don't speak in that fashion. Even if we have a sense of purpose in life, we don't talk about "coming into the world" on a mission.

Jesus said he came to fulfill the Scriptures: "Do not think that I have come to abolish the Law or the Prophets; I have not come to abolish them but to fulfill them" (Matt. 5:17)

He said he came to preach and proclaim: "Let us go somewhere else—to the nearby villages—so I can preach there also. That is why I have come." (Mark 1:30)

He said he came to lead us out of darkness: " I have come into the world as a light, so that no one who believes in me should stay in darkness." (John 12:46)

Standing before Pontius Pilate Jesus said: "You say that I am a king. In fact, the reason I was born and came into the world is to testify to the truth. " (John 18:37)

He said that he came to give life: "I have come that they may have life, and have it to the full." (John 10:10)

And as if all that were not enough, he said that he came in order to serve, and to sacrifice: "For even the Son of Man did not come to be served, but to serve, and to give his life as a ransom for many." (Mark 10:45).

There are many ways to contemplate the life-changing reality of the coming of the Son of God. In this devotional we will consider 25 key words or phrases which are associated with the birth of Jesus. We will think about joy, peace, Immanuel, shepherd, Magi, Mary, star, flesh, virgin, counselor, prince, manger, and more. In each of these words is locked a treasure.

You may read the material one reading a day, or at your own pace. If you begin on December 1, you will end on Christmas Day, but you can do the readings at any time during the Christmas season, really.

God bless you as you draw closer to Christ this year.

—Mel Lawrenz

For more, go to:
www.WordWay.org

1

JOY

But the angel said to them, "Do not be afraid. I bring
you good news of great joy that will be for all the people.
Today in the town of David a Savior has been born to
you; he is Christ the Lord."

— Luke 2:10-11

Great joy? Is it almost too much to hope for?

Where did all the Christmas joy go? How did
things get so complicated? So rushed? So squeezed
and cluttered? A nonstop buzz of Christmas lights
and weary shoppers, boisterous television specials
and pleading children. It doesn't have to be this
way. We can choose to step aside, step into a qui-
eter moment, and read the angel's words that came
on the night that changed the world: "I bring you
good news of great joy!"

It was just another night of work in the field for the shepherds, with a chill in the air and the soft bleating of their flocks. Another night of work, a night like thousands of nights before—even thousands of years before when the shepherd David was still a boy and stood watch in those same fields. Life hadn't changed in a millennium. But on this night, *everything* changed.

When the angel appeared, bathed in a glorious light, these shepherd men and boys who were used to fending off wild beasts to protect their sheep were suddenly filled with terror. Were they convinced by the simple words: "I bring you good news of great joy"? Probably not. Joy would have to come later. They would need to see proof.

That's the way it works with joy. Real joy never originates from within; it must come from without. Searching for joy within you is like searching for the ocean within a droplet of water. Perhaps this is why so many of us have a difficult time finding joy at Christmas. Bite into a Christmas cookie and you might enjoy it. Open a shiny package and you might delight in what you find inside. But joy itself—true and pure—is so much more than enjoyment.

Joy is the startling realization that God has claimed territory in this world. He has taken back what belongs to him. Every day we can remind ourselves of this revelation—reignite this joy again and again. Joy is a thirst that doesn't want to be quenched; a hunger that knows it will go on and on. It's a good thing to never get enough of God.

This "great joy"—God come into the world—is great because it's everywhere. A joy "that will be for all the people" is here. Now. Let us delight in this tremendous news today.

Prayer for today:

Dear God, turn my fear into great joy.

2

PEACE

Suddenly a great company of the heavenly host appeared with the angel, praising God and saying, "Glory to God in the highest, and on earth peace to men on whom his favor rests."

— Luke 2:13-14

Peace is a noble aspiration at any time, in times of war or in times of harmony. When you find yourself at odds with someone, or when you're feeling pretty good about your relationships. When you feel in harmony with God, or when you feel a discord. It is always important to pursue peace.

Peace is so much more than the absence of conflict. Maybe you can lay your head on your pillow tonight and thank God that you experienced no conflict, but that is not the same thing as experiencing peace. If a husband and wife get tired of shouting at each other and both slip into an icy indifference, that is not peace.

In Hebrew the word for "peace" is *shalom*, a well wishing that says it all: May you be healthy, whole, and complete. May you know where you fit in the universe, and may you find tranquility there. Augustine said peace is "the tranquility of order." When you know where you fit into God's world—that you are higher than the animals, but less than God—that is the sense of order that brings tranquility.

Therefore, we pray for peace at Christmas. We pray that we all will discover the Christmas *shalom*—the confidence that when God's favor, his undeserved grace, rests on us, we will know a peace that goes beyond understanding. The peace gifted to us because Christ came into the world and put things in order, beginning with his birth and completed in his sacrificial death and triumphant resurrection.

Prayer for today:

Dear God, let your favor rest on me, and let me stand in the peace that Christ has made possible.

3

ANGEL

An angel of the Lord appeared to him in a dream and said: "Joseph son of David, do not be afraid to take Mary home as your wife, because what is conceived in her is from the Holy Spirit. She will give birth to a son, and you are to give him the name Jesus, because he will save his people from their sins."

— Matthew 1:20-21

Angel: 1. A spiritual being believed to act as an attendant, agent, or messenger of God. (Oxford English Dictionary)

What did Mary see when the angel Gabriel appeared to her? What kind of being came with foreknowledge of a supernatural conception and with words that would change her identity forever? "Greetings, you who are highly favored! The Lord is with you" (Luke 1:28). How would the shepherds have described the angel with the glory of the Lord shining about? How could they encapsulate "a great company of the heavenly host" (Luke 2:13) whose voices poured out a sudden tidal wave of sound, a booming chorus? "Glory to God in the highest!" (Luke 2:14). How would Joseph describe his own encounter with the angel? Or what would Zechariah, John the Baptist's father, say about his angelic messenger? In the days leading up to the birth of Jesus, supernatural appearances and utterances were occurring like they never had before—an electric buzz of heaven's voices among us.

The real meaning of angel is simply "messenger." This reminds us that Christmas is about a message. It is a gospel—good news. The best news. And paving the way were powerful spiritual messengers whose very presence struck fear and awe into people. (No pudgy winged cherubs here!) Their mission and their message transformed humankind—and we have never been the same.

This year, any one of us can probably think of a dozen cases in which we'd like to hear a personal message from God. We've already received that message, however, and it is individually suited to each of us because it was sent to all of us. As the angel said to Joseph: "[Jesus] will save his people from their sins." The angel's message from that cold night continues to ring through the atmosphere. Centuries later, it is still as true as it was in its first utterance. In this mortal world that is at once full of wonders, yet seized by sin and darkness, we have been saved.

Prayer for today:

Lord, thank you for your message of hope and renewal, for your Son. Let my heart receive this message anew every day, and may my eyes be opened to your continued presence in this world.

4

VIRGIN

God sent the angel Gabriel to Nazareth, a town in Galilee, to a virgin pledged to be married to a man named Joseph, a descendant of David. The virgin's name was Mary. The angel went to her and said, "Greetings, you who are highly favored! The Lord is with you." Mary was greatly troubled at his words and wondered what kind of greeting this might be. But the angel said to her, "Do not be afraid, Mary, you have found favor with God. You will be with child and give birth to a son, and you are to give him the name Jesus."

— Luke 1:26-31

Can any of us fathom the immense amount of faith Mary was called upon to have? She was young. She was a virgin. She was probably expecting to lead no more than an ordinary life in a no-name Galilean town.

Then the message came from heaven.

To be visited by an angel would be miraculous in itself. But the words! Those powerful, surreal words: "The Lord is with you" (v. 28). Certainly that is true for all of us, generally speaking; but in this case the emphasis was: The Lord is with *you*, Mary. The Creator of the universe has handpicked "you who are highly favored." As with Abraham, Moses, Isaiah, Ruth, and David, God chose Mary to be his instrument, to do his work in the world. A high favor indeed.

"You will be with child," in a way that no woman before or since has been with child. A virgin, and yet with child. It is a difficult concept for us to grasp. Within Mary, God did something unique, which isn't too hard for him to do, but it's often very complicated for us to understand. Is it too hard for the Creator of the universe to cause a woman to have, by an act of creation, a complete zygote that would become an embryo, which would become a fetus, which would become a newborn baby? No. The virginal conception is only impossible to believe if you think the Creator can't do anything just once. But who can make up such a rule for God?

Mary is a pivotal figure worth consideration this Christmas season. She stands at the crossroads between the prophets of the Old Testament and the apostles of the New. The channel for the old prophecies to be fulfilled, and the new salvation given—the womb that carried the heavens' Prince, the woman who had faith enough to bring to term our Liberator from death.

She was asked to believe something that many of us struggle to even imagine. From that frightful day when she was face to face with a strange messenger, to the cold night in the stable, to the mournful day her son was mounted on a cross—Mary's entire life witnessed and nurtured Jesus' message.

Stop and ask yourself: *If Mary were here today, how would she celebrate Christmas?*

When you find yourself feeling lost or in despair, know that you have the same capacity for the extraordinary faith that Mary did. She was human, as you and I are. Ask yourself, *How might I fortify my faith every day? Who else inspires me with their extraordinary faith?*

Will I be prepared when a time comes for me to have great faith?

Prayer for today:

Lord, help me to trust you in the choices you make. Help me to have even a measure of the faith that Mary had.

Lord, do whatever you choose to do in my life. Let me grow stronger every day in the assurance of your message and your grace.

5

SHEPHERD

And there were shepherds living out in the fields nearby, keeping watch over their flocks at night.

— Luke 2:8

It may seem like a stretch of the imagination, but try it anyway: If you were God and could announce the arrival of the Savior of humanity, would you send your messengers to some shepherds out in the fields as they whiled away their nighttime watch? Why not send angels to an assembly of the religious council in Jerusalem instead? Why not send them to the megalomaniac King Herod? Or how about Caesar? Wouldn't that be a night of work— blowing open the doorways of society and changing everything with a few simple words?

Yet God chose the shepherds. Rough characters at that time, shepherds were laborers who performed the tedious tasks that many others were unwilling to do. They appeared ragged, smelled of the flocks, and were used to sleeping on the cold, hard ground.

Often the Bible tells us about extraordinary shepherds. A millennia earlier, David, the "shepherd king" of Israel, had cared for his people just as he'd cared for the sheep when he was a boy shepherd in the fields outside of Bethlehem. David could write the incredible words of Psalm 23 because he knew what it meant to be a good shepherd, and he knew that God was his good shepherd.

David tells us, "The Lord is my shepherd, I shall not be in want. He makes me lie down in green pastures, he leads me beside quiet waters" (vv. 1-2). And that's not all. The Lord guides (v. 3). He protects with his rod and staff (v. 4).

Jesus, the descendant of David, came to earth to be the good shepherd. In the Gospel of John, Jesus said he knows us as his sheep, and we are to know him (10:14-15). He promised to defend us from wolves and not run away. But most importantly, he said the good shepherd lays down his life for his sheep.

So consider this: On the night that Jesus' life began in this world, an inexorable process was set in motion—leading to the day when he would lay down his life for the world. All of this in the fashion of a truly good shepherd. So an angelic visitation to shepherds in Bethlehem—men who understood feeding and guiding and saving—was the best way for chapter one to begin.

Prayer for today:

The Lord is my shepherd. I shall not be in want. He makes me lie down in green pastures, he leads me beside quiet waters, he restores my soul. He guides me in paths of righteousness for his name's sake. Even though I walk through the valley of the shadow of death, I will fear no evil, for you are with me; your rod and your staff, they comfort me. You prepare a table before me in the presence of my enemies. You anoint my head with oil; my cup overflows. Surely goodness and love will follow me all the days of my life, and I will dwell in the house of the Lord forever. (Psalm 23)

6

JOSEPH

This is how the birth of Jesus Christ came about: His mother Mary was pledged to be married to Joseph, but before they came together, she was found to be with child through the Holy Spirit. Because Joseph her husband was a righteous man and did not want to expose her to public disgrace, he had in mind to divorce her quietly.

— Matthew 1:18-19

We know so little about Joseph. He is only mentioned in the birth and childhood stories of Jesus. He was named after an ancient patriarch who used his success in Egypt to save his family and a future nation. Joseph was a carpenter who lived in the town of Nazareth. His ancestors were from Bethlehem. So when a Roman ruler, Caesar Augustus, wanted to take a census, Joseph had to go back to

Bethlehem even though his wife was well along in her pregnancy.

The most important thing we know about Joseph is that when the time called for it, he displayed great faith and grace. He found out that the woman to whom he was engaged to be married was pregnant. While Mary had the benefit of an angel to explain her unique conception, Joseph had not been visited yet. All he had was Mary's word. So what was that conversation like? No, she hadn't slept with another man. Yes, she was pregnant. And yes, a spiritual being had told her she would conceive by a unique act of God. And as if that weren't enough—the child in her womb would be the Savior of the world.

Why did Joseph believe her? Why did he change his first plans to quietly divorce her so as not to expose her to public shame? (Engagements were so serious back then that to break one off amounted to getting a divorce.) If you were in his shoes, would you have believed Mary?

Here is something for all of us to think about at Christmas. Think of Joseph. Think of him looking into Mary's eyes, hearing her account, knowing in his heart of hearts it's true, and having the courage to act on that faith even though he may have had doubts. As nonsensical as it seemed, he believed it.

As much as the idea of a virginal conception violates both logic and science (even the rudimentary science of a millennia ago), Joseph knew it was possible with God. As risky as it was to stay with Mary and be branded by others as the hapless dupe of an immoral woman, Joseph decided to take that leap of faith.

That is true faith. It wasn't just that he trusted Mary. Joseph trusted God—that God could, that God might, that God would.

Prayer for today:

God, give me Joseph's courage and iron-strong faith. Give me faith to believe that, at the birth of Jesus, you really did enter this world—my world—and you're still working powerfully in it.

7

KINGDOM

"He will be great and will be called the Son of the Most High. The Lord God will give him the throne of his father David, and he will reign over the house of Jacob forever; his kingdom will never end."

— Luke 1:32-33

Christmas represents a beginning that makes sense only if we comprehend the end. The beginning is a child—a humble birth in an earthy stable. But the end... The end is an explosion of divine glory bright enough for the whole world to see— like the birth of a new star. The end is a kingdom. Jesus came to forward the kingdom of God, to open people's eyes to the power of God, to make it the central reality of their lives. "His kingdom will never end."

Now contrast Jesus' approach with King Herod's, a man who sought to protect his kingdom by trying to eliminate any potential rival to his throne. What Herod didn't understand was that by killing all of the baby boys in Bethlehem, he was not protecting his kingdom but showing its weakness and fearfulness. In the wake of God's kingdom and power, all human power is simply water dribbling through cupped hands, no matter how steadfast the grasp.

The kingdom of Christ is different; it will never end. There is no rival to his authority, though unbelievers will always abound. There is no one sitting at the right hand of God except Christ. No other authority was present when the earth was created, nor will there be one when the final judgment comes.

Christmas is a celebration of the coming of a kingdom. Powerful. Life-changing. Overwhelming. Don't ever think that Christmas is a way for us to wrap up God in a package, put a bow on it, and keep the whole thing under our control. It's not a way for us to avoid God except during those extra-special religious seasons.

The first Christmas was the arrival of a King. Rulers from the east knew it, so they came to present him with gifts. King Herod knew it, which is why he ordered all the baby boys in Bethlehem to be killed. It is the Battle of Bethlehem, the beginning of a war in which the King of kings is intent on taking back territory that belonged to him all along, and sweeping people like us into a new benevolent kingdom.

Prayer for today:

Dear God, help me to live these days with a knowledge that you are reigning in this broken world as King. Your kingdom come, your will be done, on earth as it is in heaven.

8

MANGER

She wrapped him in cloths and placed him in a manger, because there was no room for them in the inn.

— Luke 2:7

Where is a baby first placed after he or she emerges from the mother's womb? Today, we use hyper-sterilized blankets and sanitized cribs. A Plexiglas dome, if necessary. All precautions are taken to minimize the number of germs the child may come in contact with.

But Mary laid Jesus in a feeding trough for animals. The Good Shepherd took refuge that night in the sheep's manger; and when the shepherds came to see what had been announced to them, how stunned they must have been.

Of course, this would not have been Mary and Joseph's first choice. They would have preferred a modest room at a local inn, had there been any vacancies. If it all took place today, maybe a red neon light would have flashed a big NO that created a ghastly pool of light on the asphalt parking lot.

There are times when no is the hardest thing we have to hear. Yet Jesus has seen and continues to see the no sign from the very human race he had a hand in creating. Many people don't even want to consider him. Even in the life of a faithful believer, there is so much inside of us that wants to say to him, *Stay out of that part of my life. Keep that door closed. No, you may not spend the night.*

So instead, Jesus stays where he can. A feeding trough will do. He's not protected from the world, but lying in it.

Prayer for today:

Lord, make way in my heart and mind for you today. Unlock every door. Open the most valued places. Don't let me try to exclude you from any part of my life.

9

JESUS

She will give birth to a son, and you are to give him the name Jesus, because he will save his people from their sins.

— Matthew 1:21

Sometimes a name is just a name, and sometimes a name captures someone perfectly. The ancients inclined to choose names carefully, so as to make a lifelong statement about a person's identity. "Jesus" is a name so familiar to us today that we easily forget it was a name with extraordinary significance. The name an angel announced should be given to Mary and Joseph's new child. And what a name! "Jesus" means "the Lord saves."

He does indeed.

"Call him Jesus," the angel said, "because he will save his people from their sins." None of us can save ourselves anymore than a person sinking in a rowboat can save himself by pulling up on the side of the boat. We need a savior, and not just a theoretical savior, but one who really has the power of God to separate us from the tyranny and the guilt of sin.

But there wouldn't have been a saving sacrifice if there hadn't been an incarnation. Bethlehem was the start of the mission. We don't need to wait until Good Friday and Easter Sunday to celebrate the Savior. The saving started at the birth of Jesus.

Mary and Joseph could not have understood all of this, of course. They were obedient and named the newborn Jesus, "the Lord saves," but how and when the Lord would save them was still a mystery to them. Not so for us. This side of the crucifixion and resurrection of Jesus, we know the extent of the saving love of God.

Prayer for today:

Lord, make me more aware of my sins today and help me know that they shrink before the powerful person of Jesus.

10

CHRIST

Today in the town of David a Savior has been born to you; he is Christ the Lord.

— Luke 2:11

Some people think "Christ" is Jesus' last name—Jesus Christ, like Joe Johnson or Audrey Smith. If you've thought that, don't feel bad. It is just further evidence that over the centuries our understanding of Jesus as the Christ has become so solid in our thinking that we don't think of "Jesus" without "Christ."

Jesus is his name; Christ is his title. Among all of the titles he bears—Son of God, Son of Man, Good Shepherd, Alpha and Omega—it all begins in the gospel story with this one incredible announcement: "He is *Christ the Lord.*" The word is *Christos* in Greek, and thus it's *Christ* in English.

And it's *Messiah* in Hebrew, which means "Anointed One."

But what is the meaning of "Anointed One"?

In the Old Testament, three kinds of people were anointed: kings, priests, and prophets. So when we hear "Christ," we should think of Jesus in each of those three roles. He is a king who rules in people's lives not just because they are in his realm, but also because he is in their hearts. He is a priest who stands between God and humanity—one who sacrifices, one who intercedes, the mediator, the bridge. And he is a prophet too. Prophets brought the words of God to the people, but the Messiah *is* the Word of God to the people.

In those days when the heavy hand of Caesar Augustus dominated the Holy Land, people were looking for the Anointed One to come. They were hoping for a large army, not a multitude of the heavenly host. They anticipated a bigger and better David, not the obscure rabbi who always seemed like an outsider when he visited Jerusalem. They probably expected an orator, but they did not expect the speeches of this Messiah to leave people speechless.

The very best things God does in our lives usually come as a surprise to us. So wouldn't it be surprising if we, who think we know so much about

Jesus, would be startled to see him in a whole new way? We picture him in a Nativity set or as the subject of praise in hymns. We picture him in art, in stories. We experience him while reading the Bible, or while listening to a Sunday sermon. But we often fail to picture him as the living, breathing manifestation of God on earth. This, the angel said, was "good news of great joy." What could be better than God existing in the midst of our lives?

Prayer for today:

Christ, you are the King above all other kings, the high priest who made the ultimate sacrifice, the prophet who had the last word. Let me be astonished this Christmas by knowing more fully than ever before that you really have come and changed this world, and you are still here.

11

BETHLEHEM

So Joseph also went up from the town of Nazareth in Galilee to Judea, to Bethlehem the town of David, because he belonged to the house and line of David.

— Luke 2:4

Bethlehem was like any other town in the hills of Judea. And yet it was the birthplace of the greatest king of Israel, David, and one thousand years later, the Messiah.

How does such an honor come to the ordinary? Were the people of this town particularly worthy? Was there some great strategic advantage to where it lay? Were the people of Bethlehem politically savvy, having a long history of producing great leaders? Not at all. The little town of Bethlehem was in the shadow of great Jerusalem just six miles to the north. Even the meaning of Bethlehem, "house of bread," is unremarkable.

But hundreds of years before the birth of Jesus, the prophet Micah predicted the destiny of an unremarkable, small place: "But you, Bethlehem Ephrathah, though you are small among the clans of Judah, out of you will come for me one who will be ruler over Israel, whose origins are from of old, from ancient times" (Mic. 5:2).

The townspeople of Bethlehem were surely proud to be the "Town of David" and the home of King David's famous great-grandmother, Ruth. Proud also, to be the location of the tomb of Rachel, Jacob's beloved wife. Yet, they must have wondered what Micah's prophecy really meant. When would another prophet like Samuel come to town and anoint a new king, just as he had done with the boy David?

But it didn't happen that way. On an ordinary day, while men plied their trades and women baked bread and children played in the streets, a traveling couple from Nazareth arrived looking for a room. They received no special treatment. No one offered them a room. Ordinary people were having an ordinary response to an ordinary looking couple.

Honor comes to the ordinary because of God's choice, whether it is God's choice to use a town, or a nation, or even a single man or woman, boy or girl. So if this is shaping up to be an ordinary day for you—be prepared. That's the stage on which the acts of God are played.

Prayer for today:

Dear God, it so easy for us to assume that nothing exciting will happen with the ordinary. Help us this Christmas to see the amazing things you do when you choose to use the ordinary.

12

IMMANUEL

All this took place to fulfill what the Lord had said through the prophet: "The virgin will be with child and will give birth to a son, and they will call him Immanuel"—which means, "God with us."

— Matthew 1:22-23

My wife and I seriously lost track of our daughter only once. We were walking through a crowded tourist town, and the streets were lined with shops. It was evening and the crowds were dense. Suddenly, I noticed that neither my wife nor I had our eight-year-old daughter by the hand. We spun around but were unable to spot her. With candy stores beckoning children indoors, and winding side streets all around, she could be anywhere. After a few minutes of running around, I somehow spotted her far way on a side street. The look on her face was unforgettable: "Where were you?" she asked, but her eyes said, *Thank God you are with me now. I am never going to leave your side again.*

"With us." There is hardly a more central promise that God has ever made to human beings. The alternative is just too horrifying to imagine. If God has abandoned us and that is why so many bad things happen in life, then what does that say about God? What does it say about our destiny? If God oscillates in and out of our lives, willing to be with us only as long as we don't get too obnoxious, coming and going like a father who grows lax in his responsibility—where does that leave us? If God cannot be with us, then we would have to conclude that we will never reap the benefits of divine presence, and words like *grace, mercy, love,* and *truth* have no meaning.

Jesus was born but he was also sent, and Immanuel was one of his names. *Immanu-el:* "with us [is] God." "God with us." His body is among us, his message from the heavens. He turned life upside down with the divine truths he presented. But he also left people with the sense that they'd never been closer to God than when they were with him.

We don't need to stay lost. God is not indifferent to our condition. And he came to us in the most radical way, by taking our flesh, our humanity, on himself.

Prayer for today:

Dear Lord, I need to know you are with us. Help me this Christmas to know, more than I've ever known before, that you have come and that we can always live in the conscious enjoyment of your presence.

13

SOUL

"My soul glorifies the Lord and my spirit rejoices in God my Savior."

— Luke 1:46-47

One of the worst things that can happen to a person is to live with a shrunken understanding of God, a shrunken soul. This is the perfect reason to take Christmas seriously, as it is our best hope for our minds and hearts to be enlarged with God's greatness.

Mary's response to the message that she would bear the Savior was a remarkable song of praise, sometimes known as the *Magnificat* (Luke 1:46-55). It begins, "My soul glorifies the Lord," which means that because God's announcement opened her heart to him in a way that she couldn't have imagined, her soul was beginning to grasp the big-ness of God.

I remember the first time I looked through a telescope at the open sky on a cold winter evening. When I pointed it at the half-lit moon, I was stunned as mountains and plains came into fo-cus—unlike the images in the picture books I was used to. This was the real thing in real time. And now this ethereal bright disk hanging in the night sky was a real place to me. The telescope magnified its reality. The moon didn't increase, but my com-prehension of it did.

Sometimes human beings look at God as if he were a distant point of light. But when we take his Word into consideration, and if we accept it by faith, our perspective changes drastically. We see that we are living in a greater reality, with a greater God than we had imagined, and with greater pos-sibilities in our future.

Mary knew her life would never be the sa-me—and not just her life, but also the lives of countless others—because of what God was going to do. This stretched her soul, and it can stretch ours as well.

Prayer for today:

Lord, this Christmas, please give me a larger vision of who you are. May you be magnified in my soul, and may others see that you are the focus of my celebration.

14

COUNSELOR

For to us a child is born, to us a son is given, and the government will be on his shoulders. And he will be called Wonderful Counselor, Mighty God, Everlasting Father, Prince of Peace.

— Isaiah 9:6

"What is the baby's name?" The people in Bethlehem who heard about a baby being born in a stable must have stopped by to talk to Mary or Joseph. And the new parents voiced the name they had not chosen for their son: Jesus. But hundreds of years earlier, other names had already been announced for the Anointed One. Among them, Isaiah spoke of one who would be called Wonderful Counselor.

What was a "counselor" in biblical times? It was one of the roles of a king or other high official, and their task was to be wise and judicious in the face of the most difficult questions, the most complicated negotiations, and the most intractable problems. The counsel of the king was supreme, but it was not infallible. We all know there is good counsel and there is poor counsel.

The one born of a virgin would be called Wonderful Counselor. Now that is something different. The Hebrew word for *wonderful* means something out of the ordinary, clearly different, beyond human explanation. It is the knowledge described in Psalm 139:1-6,

> O Lord, you have searched me and you know me. You know when I sit and when I rise; you perceive my thoughts from afar. You discern my going out and my lying down; you are familiar with all my ways. Before a word is on my tongue you know it completely, O Lord. You hem me in—behind and before; you have laid your hand upon me. Such knowledge is too wonderful for me, too lofty for me to attain.

When we contemplate the Nativity of Jesus, we cannot help but be full of wonder. This is how God came to us, and it is wonderful because Jesus gives us an unclouded vision of what our lives are supposed to be—good counsel. He instructed us with words of wisdom. He exemplified for us what it looks like to lead a life devoted to the Father. Yet, how often do we really heed this treasured counsel? How might we live more consciously in light of the example he set forth?

Prayer for today:

Lord, I need your counsel in every area of my life. As I think about my family, friends, work, and decisions—I know I need to be smart. So please help me listen to you this Christmas as the only One who is the Wonderful Counselor.

15

GOVERNMENT

For to us a child is born, to us a son is given, and the government will be on his shoulders. And...of the increase of his government and peace there will be no end. He will reign on David's throne and over his kingdom, establishing and upholding it with justice and righteousness from that time on and forever.

— Isaiah 9:6-7

Government. Does that word strike a positive note in you or a negative note? The word has good and bad connotations. Over the centuries, many corrupt governments run by greedy and power-hungry people have imposed tyranny rather than justice. Their form of order is more often a form of chaos.

It's a shame that government has gotten such a bad name—because it is, at the same time, a necessary function of any society hoping to be civilized. The ungoverned life is chaos, anarchy, and injustice. Without governing, people would not volunteer to pitch in for the common good, and they would be unwilling to enact laws that require them to sacrifice and set limits on their lives. And so government is a necessary constraint on our impulses and independence, a way for a person to say, "I need to have standards in my life, and I know that my neighbors and I need to live under those standards for them to be meaningful."

God knows we need governing. That's why he calls himself King, Shepherd, Master, Lord, and Father. And when Jesus was born in Bethlehem, the world gained its greatest governor.

Have you ever considered a governing individual and wondered how he or she can bear the sheer weight of immense responsibility? Yet, governing—real, life-shaping authority—ultimately rests on Christ's shoulders alone: "The government will be on his shoulders." Now, there is a future time when Jesus will reign as undisputed ruler; but in the meantime, he is exercising considerable governing power. Since that night in Bethlehem, the world has changed. It is not that evil has disappeared, but its counter—the power of Christ—has been triumphant in one life after another. We see it in the person who gains victory over an addiction, in someone who stands up for justice, in reconciled relationships, in people whose characters are being shaped by the character of Christ.

We can thank God this Christmas that he did not leave us to our chaotic, ungoverned state. A shepherd-king came to stand in the Davidic line not to be like other kings, but to govern our lives from the inside out, as he changes our hearts and enlivens our consciences.

Prayer for today:

Lord, I confess that there is much in me that does not want to be governed. Help me to see joy in the fact that your governing will never end and, because of that, peace will increase.

16

MIGHTY GOD

And he will be called...Mighty God.

— Isaiah 9:6

In the Old Testament, some of the prophecies about Christ are mysterious statements. They were so bold and so large that they were treasured through the generations until they were fulfilled and finally understood. Isaiah's oracle about a son who would be born—Wonderful Counselor, Prince of Peace, and all the rest—was one of those landmark prophecies. In that moment of inspiration, Isaiah revealed Jesus would be Mighty God.

After Jesus' life, death, resurrection, and ascension, his followers would piece together what he said and did, and they would conclude that Jesus really was one with God the Father in a way that is appropriate to call him divine. The doctrine of the

Trinity would be defined later, but in Isaiah's prophecy about the coming one are the seeds of this truth.

In the Jewish tradition, nothing was more important than belief in the "oneness" of God. Not two gods, not a thousand gods, but one and only one God. So what could happen when, in Bethlehem, Magi from the east came bearing gifts fit for a king but also worshipped him? Why did Jesus allow fishermen in a boat to worship him after he calmed a storm? Or what about Mary falling at Jesus' feet and worshiping him there in the garden after his resurrection? Or the disciple Thomas falling at his feet and saying, "My Lord and my God"?

Nobody at the start of Jesus' life, nor during his adult ministry, even hinted at anything suggesting there is more than one God. But because of who God is; because God is higher than human comprehension; because God said "us" from the very beginning: "Let us make man in our image" (Gen. 1:26); and because the coming one would be called Immanuel, "God with us" (Matt. 1:22-23), we can believe that Christmas represents the true entry of God into human affairs. The same God who created humanity also took humanity on himself when it suited his purposes—to save that same humanity.

The God who created the world entered it through a human birth in the town of Bethlehem. Not any kind of god would do that. Only the One, true, Mighty God.

Prayer for today:

Lord, I believe you are mighty. I believe you can do whatever you wish. I believe you came in the flesh in Jesus.

17

EVERLASTING FATHER

And he will be called...Everlasting Father.

— Isaiah 9:6

W hat a remarkable string of names in Isaiah 9:6! Wonderful Counselor, Mighty God, Everlasting Father, Prince of Peace.

Now, these were radical statements indeed, and they described the one who was coming to rule heaven and earth. A coming ruler might—if he were an ordinary ruler—simply assert his authority and prerogatives as sovereign. As we well know, a king is one who has the power because he has an army, and he is the one who has wealth because he controls the resources of his realm. That is the way of earthly rulers. But Isaiah also spoke of a ruler whom people would look to in far more personal terms: "Father."

But Jesus would be no mere earthly ruler. His reign would be "everlasting." Enduring, unstoppable, without challenge, having the qualities of heaven. An everlasting ruler would have to be a divine king.

It is a different kind of king who reigns as father. A king (or, for that matter, a prime minister, a president, etc.) does not have to treat his subjects as though he were their father. He can wield power simply because he has it. But a ruler who cares for those in his realm, who truly wants to protect and provide for his subjects out of a familial kind of love is as much a father as he is a king.

Hundreds of years before his birth, Jesus was called "Everlasting Father" because his reign would be about protecting and providing—a king, yes, but a fatherly one. And we should not forget that Jesus' relationship with God the Father was so close that Jesus could say: "Anyone who has seen me has seen the Father" (John 14:9).

In some parts of the world, Santa Claus is called "Father Christmas." At its best, the legend, which is derived from the story of St. Nicholas, expresses the belief in someone who is bigger than life and full of benevolence and magical charm. That Everlasting Father exists. Nothing can compare to the reality that Jesus Christ has become—for the world—the Powerful Protector and Perfect Provider, a King whose authority is so right and so good, it will never end.

Born a child, destined to bring fatherly care. Always and forever. In this, the children of God place their faith and hope.

Prayer for today:

Lord, help me to fully submit to your authority as King in my life, and then let me know your protection and provision which goes beyond what any earthly father can provide.

18

PRINCE

And he will be called...Prince of Peace.

— Isaiah 9:6

In ancient times, princes, whether they desired it or not, often became warriors. Rulers of nations may talk about peace, but nothing is more elusive than peace. And so, when Isaiah talked about a child who would be born, a son who would be given, one who would be called "Prince of Peace," it sounded like high rhetoric, wishful thinking. Could it ever happen?

When you look at the life of Jesus, it hardly appears to be a life of peace. He was in constant conflict with people who had invented their own ideas about God, and with people who didn't want God to meddle in their affairs at all. Jesus had enemies. In the end he died a most violent death, which was preceded by humiliating abuse. His followers were harassed and persecuted. Fishermen died as martyrs.

Yet, it is in Jesus' sacrifice that he became Prince of Peace. Only when the chief enemies of humanity—sin, death, evil—were defeated could people live in peace with God, with themselves, and with the world.

And so, yes, he was the Prince of Peace. The angel was right in saying "Glory to God in the highest, and on earth peace..."(Luke 2:14). The apostle Paul offered a sincere blessing of peace when he said: "Now may the Lord of peace himself give you peace at all times and in every way" (2 Thess. 3:16).

This is the kind of prince—a ruler brand-new to the world—that the prophecies described. So when we think of Bethlehem, we must remember that it was not the stable that made this baby unique, nor the virtues of Mary or Joseph, nor the angelic presence, nor any other feature of those extraordinary days—as important as they are. The child was remarkable because Jesus is the only Prince to truly bring a lasting peace—a peace that has lasted for millennia, and will last into eternity.

Where do you need to find peace in your life at this time? Your family? Your workplace? Your inner life? We can be assured of this: God is for peace and reconciliation, and God wants to bring order where there has been chaos in our lives.

Prayer for today:

Lord, I know there will be battles in my life, and I know that some fights between what is right and wrong are necessary. But help me to live in the calm and confidence that you have made it possible for me to live at peace with you.

19

MAGI

After Jesus was born in Bethlehem in Judea, during the time of King Herod, Magi from the east came to Jerusalem and asked, "Where is the one who has been born king of the Jews? We saw his star in the east and have come to worship him."

— Matthew 2:1-2

Mary and Joseph stayed in Bethlehem many months after the birth of Jesus, yet we know nothing about that time. How was Mary treating her baby, knowing she would have to submit to him as her Lord? How much attention were they getting from the townspeople? What were they telling people, if anything? We simply don't know. But we do know that one day some travelers from the east—maybe from Persia or Mesopotamia (the regions of modern day Iran or Iraq)—suddenly showed up in Bethlehem, claiming to have been guided to a new king by a star.

The word *Magi* refers to people who belonged to a priestly caste that focused on special knowledge, interpretation of dreams, and astrology. Despite popular depictions, they were not kings. We don't know their names, and we don't know for certain that there were three of them. (That is a tradition inferred from the fact that they bore three gifts: gold, incense, and myrrh.) There may have been two; there may have been twelve.

But what we *do* know of them is startling. They saw a sign. They were motivated. They traveled. No wonder they are sometimes called "wise men." They were not merely astrologers. They were worshipers. Jerusalem was their first stop where they inquired about a new king (which is a sure way to set off an alarm for the existing king); but then they found Bethlehem. They delivered their valuable gifts and they bowed in worship. If people in Bethlehem weren't paying much attention in the months following the birth of Jesus, they surely were now.

Though foreign to this land, Jesus was of keen interest to them. These stories remind us that we can often overlook the miracles taking place in our own neighborhoods. If we aren't careful, the celebration of Christmas can become so familiar to us that we let it come and go without taking time to truly contemplate the miracles and blessings we celebrate each season. Men from the Far East went out of their way to find Christ and set treasures before him. Would it take strangers to remind us of the blessings in our midst too?

One of the best things we can do in this retail-obsessed Christmas season is bring the gift of worship to him.

Prayer for today:

Lord, I know that what you want me to give you is my life. Help me with my motivation, with my willingness to go the distance. Show me what gifts I can bring you.

20

STAR

They went on their way, and the star they had seen in the east went ahead of them until it stopped over the place where the child was. When they saw the star, they were overjoyed.

— Matthew 2:9-10

In Psalm 19, David gives voice to the stars:

> The heavens declare the glory of God; the skies proclaim the work of his hands. Day after day they pour forth speech; night after night they display knowledge. There is no speech or language where their voice is not heard. Their voice goes out into all the earth, their words to the ends of the world. (vv. 1-4)

If you've ever stood outside and looked up at the canopy of stars—away from the city, away from noise—you may have seen that the stars have a message. In silence they speak, and their voice is thunderous.

The star of Bethlehem, a sign in the sky noted by the Magi, may have been a miraculous event matching the miraculous entry of the Savior into the world. Or it may have been a natural astronomical phenomenon that God used as a sign. In either case, the heavens were speaking in a unique way about a unique world-changing event. Should that come as any surprise?

But note that only the observant recognized the sign, and in this case they were outsiders. God drew outsiders toward Bethlehem with a word he placed in the sky. Don't ever doubt that God is speaking to the "outsider" and that those who seek will find. Christmas is both for believers and for those who have yet to come to faith. In those days, it was a celestial sign that attracted the attention of outsiders. Today, there are many signs that Jesus accomplished something unique in the world, acts that arise out of and point to his holy character.

Prayer for today:

Lord, thank you for putting your clear markers into this world and into our lives so we can know that you are real and what you intend to do. May this Christmas be a new marker for me.

21

FLESH

The Word became flesh and made his dwelling among us.
— John 1:14

Not only did the Son of God become a baby, but he also became flesh. Divinity joined to corporeal muscle, blood, and bones. In this humbling of the eternal Son of God, the Word who was with God from the beginning, and who was God, chose to begin in the way all flesh does—as a newborn.

But what does *flesh* really mean? Doesn't it sound a bit crass?

In the Bible, the word *flesh* points to a number of different realities. Literally, it means "the body," the tissues and bones and fluids that are common to any human being living anywhere in the world at any time. The body is the jar of clay in which God has placed treasures. Consequently, at another

level, *flesh* can mean "humanity" or "human nature." To speak of "flesh and blood" refers to the
humanness that you share with your family,
friends, and people you've never met. And at a different level, *flesh* can mean "fallen, flawed, human."
"The flesh" is shorthand in Paul's epistles for in-
trinsic human nature—broken and fallible.

But there is one exception. One human life that
was not flawed and full of sin—Jesus'.

"The word became flesh." It means that the Son
of God became human—really, truly human—with
the exception that he had no sin. Christmas is a
time of awe because it marks the best news the
human race ever received: our Creator had so
much love for us that he joined the human race in
order to save it. He is a Savior who experienced
real hunger, real fatigue, real sorrow. He faced
temptation when the evil one tempted him in the
wilderness with very "fleshy" things like power,
wealth, and authority (Luke 4:1-13).

Jesus knows us because he was one of us. Real
flesh, but perfect. So on those days when we're so
disappointed with ourselves because we're having
a hard time controlling the flesh, this is the kind of
Savior we must turn to.

Prayer for today:

Lord, help me to hear "the Word" this Christmas. Help me to see you for who you are in all your glory. Thank you for humbling yourself.

22

LIGHT

---

*For my eyes have seen your salvation, which you have
prepared in the sight of all people, a light for revelation
to the Gentiles and for glory to your people Israel.*

— Luke 2:30-32

The winter solstice on December 21 is the darkest
day of the year. For those of us who live halfway
between the equator and the North Pole, that
means we eat breakfast when it's still dark outside,
and by suppertime the sun has long set. That slide
toward the shortest day of the year seems like sinking into a black hole. No wonder people in ancient
cultures celebrated the days when the sun began to
return. The prophet Malachi spoke of the healing
power of light: "The sun of righteousness will rise
with healing in its wings" (Mal. 4:2).

Eight days after Jesus' birth, Mary and Joseph took him to the temple as the law required. A man named Simeon saw Jesus, and his eyes were opened to the reality of Jesus' identity. His eyes saw God's salvation. There, in human form. Simeon was at the right place, at the right time. And Jesus was brought to earth not by royalty, but by an ordinary couple. Simeon saw in Jesus a brilliant light that would show the way to salvation—not just for Israel, but for all nations.

The days were dark then. It was hard to know when deliverance from the tight grip of the Romans might come. Roman taxation was heavy; the sight of soldiers in the streets was a constant insult; war was always just a rumor away. The occupiers built unfamiliar buildings. It was difficult to settle into a normal pattern of living when on a whim, an emperor in a faraway land could demand a census that sent you packing your bags.

The days are dark now as well. Not just because it is late December, but because more and more generations are turning their backs on faith; because wars rage on; because so many families are losing their homes and their jobs; because every day the evening news delivers more stories about murder, disaster, rape, and abuse.

But even in so much darkness, the light will never be forgotten. Light is not an illusion; in fact, darkness has no real substance. It is nothing more than the absence of light.

We need to see salvation as Simeon did—here and now. We need to use this Christmas to look at the One who has been "prepared in the sight of all people" (Luke 2:31). The public Savior; the beacon for the world; the light for revelation.

Prayer for today:

Lord, open my eyes as Simeon's eyes were opened to the Lord Jesus. Help me to see your light that I may live in truth and comfort in this dark world. And help me reflect your light to the many needy people around me.

23

BEGINNING

---

*That which was from the beginning, which we have
heard, which we have seen with our eyes, which we have
looked at and our hands have touched—this we proclaim
concerning the Word of life. The life appeared; we have
seen it and testify to it, and we proclaim to you the eternal life, which was with the Father and has appeared to
us.*

— 1 John 1:1-2

Beginning. *The* Beginning. How much we all want
to know about the beginning of all things, in order
to understand the now of all things, and to pursue
the way things are supposed to be in our lives today. The original design must be the ideal, the way
things ought to be. "In the beginning, God created
the heavens and the earth" (Gen. 1:1). The Bible's
opening words delineate between a time in which

there was only God, and a new time in which his magnificent creation began.

The opening words of the Gospel of John place the Son of God right there—at the beginning: "In the beginning was the Word, and the Word was with God, and the Word was God" (John 1:1).

Unlike any other birth, the birth of Jesus was not the beginning of a new life. Rather, one who was there in The Beginning appeared among his creation through his birth. "The life appeared; we have seen it and testify to it, and we proclaim to you the eternal life, which was with the Father and has appeared to us" (1 John 1:2). This appearance was no dream or vision or apparition, it was an extended visitation, a flood of revelation, an appearance of the Everlasting in terrestrial form, a real life. "The life appeared." It was heard; it was seen; it was felt. Bethlehem was not the beginning of the life of Christ, and that's why his life can change our lives. Jesus said: "Before Abraham was born, I AM" (John 8:58).

"I AM": I always was, I am now, and I will always be. That is why Jesus can connect us with our original purpose.

God reached out to the human race in a new way in Bethlehem. Whereas in the past God spoke through the words of prophets, a new channel of

God's communication was opened in Bethlehem. God "has spoken to us by his Son, whom he appointed heir of all things, and through whom he made the universe. The Son is the radiance of God's glory and the exact representation of his being, sustaining all things by his powerful word" (Heb. 1:2-3).

So Christmas is about the good beginning (Genesis 1), and it is about the rescue of the now (John 1). That means Jesus will help us regain everything a human life was supposed to be in the first place—a real relationship with God, real wisdom, real character, real virtue. He intends to restore the image of God in our humanness.

Prayer for today:

Lord, I acknowledge that you are the only one who can begin something new in my life. Thank you for the appearance of Jesus, the Life. Help me be a true disciple.

24

EVE

While they were there, the time came for the baby to be born.

— Luke 2:6

On the night before Jesus was born, the shepherds would have seen the night sky the way they'd seen it thousands of times before. It was a quiet night, in stark contrast to the following night when an angel would appear with the glory of the Lord, announcing the birth of the child—a great company of heavenly beings proclaiming glory and peace.

On the night before Christmas in the year 1968, three men looked into the night sky also, but from an entirely different perspective. Frank Borman, Jim Lovell, and William Anders, the crew of Apollo 8, were further away from the Earth than any human had ever been. It was the first time a spacecraft had broken Earth's orbit and ventured out one quarter of a million miles to orbit the moon. In a historic television broadcast on that Christmas Eve, the astronauts beamed back to Earth a video picture of a small blue disk, the Earth, and spoke of the "vast loneliness" of space. Then, William Anders' voice crackled over the radio: "In the beginning, God created the heaven and the earth. And the earth was without form, and void; and darkness was upon the face of the deep..."

There, on that small blue circle, the entire drama of human history has unfolded: the Creation, the fall, war, exploration, feast and famine, marriage and divorce, birth and death. And to that blue circle God came, at just the right time, to begin to make things right in the human race.

Wherever you are, whatever you are doing, Christmas Eve is a time when we approach that dividing line in human history, the doorway from BC to AD, the revolution begun by the Son of God's entry into the world. Sometimes you know when you're on the eve of something big (your wedding, moving to a new home, adopting a child), and sometimes you don't. Every Christmas Eve, we know we are about to mark the moment when Immanuel came.

So on the night before Christmas, find a quiet moment when you can think about what was about to happen in Bethlehem so many years ago. Think about all the ways you need someone to be your savior—someone who has the strength, the wisdom, the virtue that you know you cannot come up with on your own.

Prayer for today:

God, thank you that, along with millions of other people around the world, I can anticipate and celebrate the moment when you joined yourself to the human race to offer us our only hope for salvation.

25

CHRISTMAS

The shepherds returned, glorifying and praising God for all the things they had heard and seen, which were just as they had been told.

— Luke 2:20

At the birth of Jesus, amidst the dirt and straw of a stable, a millennia of promises, prophecies, and hopes were fulfilled. In the birth of a child, something that happens every single day all over the world, something happened that would change the world. Everything the faithful were anticipating took shape. It was the alignment of all that was meant to be.

The shepherds heard, they saw, and it was all just as they'd been told. In a perfect conjunction of heaven and earth, God came to earth, connecting the two for his eternal purposes. Years later, Jesus would tell us in so many different ways, "I have come into the world as a light" (John 12:46); "I have come that they may have life, and have it to the full" (John 10:10); "For this reason I was born, and for this I came into the world, to testify to the truth" (John 18:37).

So...

When we are sensing the dirtiness of life in this world, we can focus on the purity of Christ.

When we feel weak, we can lean on the power of Christ.

When we are ill, we can remember that he is the Great Physician.

When we are confused, we can turn to his words to get our bearings.

When we are damaged, we can remember that he said he would not break a bruised reed nor snuff out a smoldering wick.

When we know we have sinned, we can know his forgiveness.

When we are wayward, we can remember he called himself "the way."

When we have been lied to, we can remember he called himself "the truth."

When we feel like our energy and our enthusiasm is waning, we can remember that he called himself "the life."

And so, we can pray:

Thank you, Lord Christ, for humbling yourself and taking the form of man. Thank you for pushing back the darkness of this world and of my life. Thank you for living before us so we can see just how much life we can have. Let me live for the next 52 weeks in the light of your ongoing presence and power in this world. And then let me celebrate Christmas again—with joy.

SUPPLEMENT
"PUTTING ON FLESH"

Excerpt (chapter 11) from *Putting the Pieces Back Together: How Real Life and Real Faith Connect* by Mel Lawrenz (Zondervan, 2005)

> If God had a name what would it be?
> And would you call it to his face?
> If you were faced with him in all his glory
> What would you ask if you had just
> one question?....
> What if God was one of us?
>
> from Joan Osborne's song "One of Us"

He shouldn't have gone out in the ice storm on that cold day in 1841 even for his own inauguration as President of the United States, and certainly not without hat or coat. And he shouldn't have given a ponderous 8,495-word inaugural address that took almost two hours to deliver. But that's what sixty-eight-year-old Henry Harrison did. He developed pneumonia and died a month later, holding the shortest presidential term in history. He accomplished nothing of what he aspired to in his address.

I have often wondered what it must be like to be inaugurated into some high office, say, that of Prime Minister or President, and to know that you had a limited amount of time in which to accomplish something of significance. The inauguration of a President of the United States, for instance, is an opportunity for a whole nation, and other nations of interest, to take an accounting of all the problems that need to be fixed and the new initiatives to be taken. Some pieces put back together and other pieces put together for the very first time. How would you prevent being overwhelmed by all that needed attention? Wouldn't high-minded words of lofty aspirations seem like so much wishful thinking? Within days reality would hit, and the push and pull of all the human contests and conflicts would take over.

Maybe that's why some inaugurations have been extraordinarily simple, such as Thomas Jefferson's talk before a few close friends indoors before he retired to Conrad's Tavern to eat his dinner alone. Or the party at the White House at Andrew

Jackson's big day with common folks breaking crystal, muddying the carpets, and spitting tobacco juice on the floor. (The hosts did regain control by moving tubs of liquor onto the back lawn after Jackson had escaped by jumping out a back window.) By contrast, the Presidential inauguration in 2000 included sixty-two balls, and a $40 million price tag.

George Washington's first inaugural address focused simply on two things: his own inadequacies for the task of presidential office and the importance of acknowledging the providence of God and the necessity of God's guidance for the future. His second inaugural address was just 135 words long and took two minutes to deliver.

One has to be careful what one promises to accomplish.

If *christos*, meaning Anointed One (*messhiach*, Messiah, in Hebrew), is an office of sorts, what was Jesus claiming to accomplish when he let people conclude that he was exactly that Anointed One?

The human race knew that the Anointed One was coming. He simply had to come, being the kind of God that he is. He is good, and he is great. He must have some escape route for us, some healing power for our misery.

To hear that "God became flesh" is at once one of the most shocking claims you will ever hear, and one of the most obvious. We knew that he was coming because he is a saving kind of God.

So, long before Christ did come, people imagined in their storytelling a day when God, or one of the gods, might come to earth. He might even suffer and die. And, certainly he would rise up from death. The existence of numerous such stories or myths does not take anything away from Jesus' Incarnation; they emphasize it. It is a truth so obvious it echoes through history—across civilizations and deep in the heart even of those who have never heard the proclamation that God has come. Now and again, even today someone will discover a primitive tribe which expects that some kind of divine savior will come.

Why God Became Man

He had to come. We knew he would.

In the 11th century, a wise Christian by the name of Anselm wrote a small book called *Cur Deus Homo* (*Why God Became Man*), and in it he offered a straightforward interpretation of salvation. Anselm said that only man *should* solve the problem of sin-but only God *could*. Who ought to suffer the consequences for the mistakes and crimes of human beings? Human beings, of course. But the problem is, we cannot really pay for our own sins. We were designed as creatures of perfect goodness and nobility. So every failing, every negligence, every assault against another person puts us deeper and deeper into a moral deficit. No one can make up for all that.

No one, that is, except God.

Only man should solve the problem of sin, but only God could. And so God became man. Now Christians don't believe this because it is a neat, logical solution. It is, rather, because of the whole eye-opening, mind-blowing, assumption-shattering experience we have had with Jesus Christ since he came. Jesus' claims about why he came, in other words, have proven true many times over in the lives of countless human beings from almost every culture in the world.

The beloved disciple, John, explained it this way (John 1): "In the beginning was the Word, and the Word was with God, and the Word was God." And then, "The Word became flesh, and made his dwelling among us. We have seen his glory, the glory of the One and Only, who came from the Father, full of grace and truth." Elsewhere John talks about the truth that most gripped his life, a reality that bonded him to men and women with whom he would have nothing in common otherwise. "That which was from the beginning, which we have heard, which we have seen with our eyes, which we have looked at and our hands have touched—this we proclaim concerning the Word of life. The life appeared to us.... We write this to make our joy complete" (1 John 1). John also says, "Every spirit that acknowledges that Jesus Christ has come in the flesh is from God, but every spirit that does not acknowledge Jesus is not from God" (1 John 4).

The Incarnation was not a divine visitation in the mere form of a human being. Jesus was no holograph of divinity. Some ancient self-described sophisticates called the Gnostics, who wanted to make Christianity more spiritual than it already was, said that the Savior only appeared human and to possess real flesh. He was a super-spiritual being who came to impart cryptic saving knowledge. If you could understand this coded truth and grasp the lingo, then you would be enlightened, and thus saved by the knowledge. They even said that the Savior went nowhere near the cross. He switched identities with Simon of Cyrene, the man who was forced to carry Jesus' cross, and then stood at a distance, laughing at the foolish Romans who thought they had nailed the man who claimed to be Messiah to the cross.

But the Gnostics of ancient days and today are wrong. The Messiah didn't laugh on that day because he fooled people into thinking he was a human being, while he skirted around the torture of the cross. Rather, he took the pain of the world on himself, and in that abject agony offered the way out for us. As wrong and unjust and inexcusable as it was, the death of Jesus also makes perfect sense. It all fits into a consistent pattern of God's character, the nature of the corrupt world, and the love that God has for those he created in his own image. All the pieces fit. The mission to put the world back together was itself coming together. God was doing what only God could do.

There are many others who easily see Jesus as a man, but deny any possibility that he was divine. This should not surprise us. The Incarnation is a truth that exceeds our comprehension. It breaks the rules of the way we think things always are. Try explaining to a five-year-old that the sun, which we all know so well, is one star among millions in our galaxy, and that our galaxy, like a small cloud in the blackness, is only one among millions of other galaxies and that it all stretches to billions of light-years, and you'll see the line of comprehension crossed quite quickly. So I, for one, am not at all surprised that the truth that divinity became flesh, the Word became Jesus, the Son became son of a carpenter, exceeds the processing power of the little computer inside my skull, which can't even comprehend the properties of a single atom.

No one who believes in the Incarnation should suppose that we can get into Jesus' head and understand his coexisting divinity and humanity. We can barely understand our own inner lives. There is no special psychology text that has been written about it, and there never will be.

Who Christ Is

Now this is what Christians since the earliest days have said about the person of Christ: First, he is clearly one person, not some dualistic oddity. But in that one person there are definitely two full and distinct natures. Jesus was truly human—not just a body with divinity replacing human nature. And he was truly divine—not just a prophet or even a super-prophet who was invested with an extraordinary measure of divine power.

How do we know this? First, because he demonstrated the unique *attributes of deity*. Power when wind and waves obeyed him and when he took a dead little girl by the hand and she woke up. Holiness, glory, and omniscience. "Come, see a man who told me everything I ever did. Could this be the Christ?" (John 4:29)

Second, because he exercised the *prerogatives of deity*. He wielded authority in calling himself "the Lord of the Sabbath," and by saying astounding things such as "Heaven and earth will pass away, but my words will never pass away." He forgave people their sins. Who but God can do that? Which is why, when Jesus told a paralytic man that he forgave his sins, Jesus' opponents snarled, "Why does this fellow talk like that? He's blaspheming! Who can forgive sins but God alone?" They had no idea how right they were. Jesus said elsewhere that he would be involved in judgment ("When the Son of Man comes in his glory... he will separate the people one from another as a shepherd separates the sheep from the goats."). He solicited faith in himself: "I am the way and the truth and the life. No one comes to the Father except through me." And, most remarkable of all, he let other people worship him—the disciples in the boat after he calmed the storm, Mary in the garden after the resurrection, and even when the Magi came to worship him as a child in Bethlehem.

Now what does "worship" in these contexts mean? In the boat Jesus' disciples had no hymnals, no guitars, no offering plates. What they did have was themselves, and the ability to bow down or bend the knee in the presence of one they recognized as Lord supreme. They were compelled to do it. Bowing was as quick a response as when you squint or put your hand up when you step from a dark room out into the blazing sun. Later they must have pondered the significance of this impulse to worship a man they were following.

Third, the statements Jesus made amounted to *claims of deity.* "I and the Father are one." "Anyone who has seen me has seen the Father." "All that belongs to the Father is mine." His opponents began considering murder because "not only was he breaking the Sabbath, but he was even calling God his own Father, making himself equal with God."

And, fourth, he used *names of deity.* "Before Abraham was born, I am" (which recalls the special name God used with Moses, "I AM WHO I AM.") Thomas fell at Jesus' feet after he knew he had risen from the dead, exclaiming, "My Lord and my God!" When people called Jesus "Lord," it seemed to go well beyond the meaning of "master." There was "Son of God" and "Son of Man," both labels that expectant Jews knew identified the coming Messiah.

So during the brief earthly ministry of Jesus, his disciples gained an accumulating picture of who

Jesus of Nazareth really was. Plenty of evidence pointed to the fact that he was not just from Nazareth. He came from God's place and with a divine mission, and it was getting more astounding all the time. Jesus' disciples strained to add up all the pieces of evidence in the immediacy of the events. Like a giant puzzle, the pieces came together, but it would take time for people to step back far enough from the puzzle and see the picture in the pieces.

What is the sum of it all? C. S. Lewis put it this way in *Mere Christianity*: "I am trying here to prevent anyone saying the really foolish thing that people often say about Him: 'I'm ready to accept Jesus as a great moral teacher, but I don't accept His claim to be God.' A man who was merely a man and said the sort of things Jesus said would not be a great moral teacher. He would either be a lunatic—on a level with a man who says he is a poached egg—or else he would be the Devil of Hell. You must make your choice. Either this man was, and is, the Son of God; or else a madman or something worse."

What was Jesus trying to accomplish? The answer to that question is bound up in the person Jesus is. He was able to do what he did because of the person he is. He made an exodus for people, a way out of entanglements with self, the heavy gravity of sin, and the assassination plots of the Evil One.

And he didn't just try to pull it off. It all worked. He was there at the beginning when God said, let us make a universe, and then rested. He was there on the cross when he committed his spirit to his Father, but only after saying, "It is finished." And the "it" was an agenda that from his inauguration he was uniquely capable of fulfilling, the salvation of the shattered human race.

Pray This

Lord Jesus, you said that you will bless those who do not see you and yet still believe. So I count myself blessed. I am grateful that I can read your teachings and hear the testimony of those who saw your miraculous acts. Teach me to know you as the living Word, and help me to understand the full meaning that you came and took on human nature. Thank you for doing that out of your love for those you created.

Do you ever wish you understood the Bible better?

Almost everyone does. Mature believers and new believers. Young and old. Those who have read the Bible for years and those just starting out.

How to Understand the Bible: A Simple Guide, will help you gain an overall perspective on the flow and meaning of Scripture. It addresses questions like: What is the big picture of the Bible? What about Bible translations? How should we understand the stories of the Old Testament? How should we interpret what the prophets had to say? How should we understand the teachings of Jesus? What was Jesus teaching in the parables? How can we hear God's voice in Scripture? What are the proper ways to apply Scripture to life today?

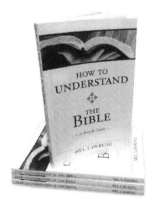

WWW.WORDWAY.ORG

For more resources:

www.WordWay.org
and
www.TheBrookNetwork.org

Facebook: thebrooknetwork
Twitter: mellawrenz

Made in the USA
Lexington, KY
26 November 2017